DALE EARNHARDT JR.

RACE CAR LEGENDS

COLLECTOR'S EDITION

Jeff Burton

Dale Earnhardt Jr.

Famous Finishes

Famous Tracks

Kenny Irwin Jr.

Jimmie Johnson

The Labonte Brothers

Lowriders

Monster Trucks & Tractors

Motorcycles

Off-Road Racing

Rockcrawling

Tony Stewart

The Unsers

Rusty Wallace

DALE EARNHARDT JR.

Bill Fleischman

CHELSEA HOUSE
PUBLISHERS

Cover Photo: Dale Earnhardt Jr. celebrates in victory lane at the Talladega Superspeedway after winning the EA Sports 500 on October 6, 2002 in Talladega, Alabama.

CHELSEA HOUSE PUBLISHERS

VP, New Product Development   Sally Cheney
Director of Production   Kim Shinners
Creative Manager   Takeshi Takahashi
Manufacturing Manager   Diann Grasse

STAFF FOR DALE EARNHARDT JR.

Editorial Assistant Sarah Sharpless
Production Editor Bonnie Cohen
Photo Editor Pat Holl
Series Design and Layout Hierophant Publishing Services/EON PreMedia

© 2006 by Chelsea House Publishers.

http://www.chelseahouse.com

First Printing

1   3   5   7   9   8   6   4   2

Library of Congress Cataloging-in-Publication Data

Fleischman, Bill.
    Dale Earnhardt, Jr. / Bill Fleischman.
        p. cm.—(Race car legends. Collector's edition)
    Includes bibliographical references and index.
    ISBN 0-7910-8671-2
    1. Earnhardt, Dale, Jr.—Juvenile literature. 2. Stock car drivers—
United States—Biography—Juvenile literature. I. Title. II. Series.
GV1032.E18F44 2005
796.72'092—dc22

                                                                    2005010415

TABLE OF CONTENTS

① A SHINING STAR

He is the "rock star" of the National Association for Stock Car Racing (NASCAR). Dale Earnhardt Jr. is as comfortable hanging out with rock musicians and Hollywood stars as he is racing cars at 180 miles per hour. Even before he emerged as arguably NASCAR's most popular younger driver, Earnhardt signed a megabucks contract with the Anheuser-Busch brewery as his team sponsor. Back then he was billed as "the rising son." Now, the son of Dale Earnhardt Sr. has risen and is shining brightly.

Earnhardt earns an estimated $20 million each year from such sponsors as Budweiser beer, Wrangler jeans, Drakkar-Noir cologne, Enterprise Rental Car, Kraft Foods, NAPA auto products and Spy sunglasses. The value of the Budweiser deal with Anheuser-Busch was estimated at $10 million annually when it was negotiated in 1998. Don Hawk, the former president of Dale Earnhardt Inc., arranged the deal with Anheuser-Busch. Referring to Dale Jr.'s future popularity, Hawk said, "We're sitting on a keg of dynamite."[1] How wise he was . . . Looking back on the deal, when he was racing Friday and Saturday nights on Carolina dirt tracks, Junior smiled and said, "[Back then] we couldn't even raise 20 grand to run."[2] The Anheuser-Busch contract was renewed in 2004.

Dale Earnhardt Jr. stands on pit road, awaiting his turn at qualifying for a NASCAR race at the Texas Motor Speedway in Fort Worth, Texas. A famous name only gets you so far—NASCAR's "rising son" has performed well under the extra scrutiny he gets for being a race car legend's son.

To illustrate how big Earnhardt is, he was featured in two commercials during the 2004 Super Bowl game. Only Muhammad Ali has also appeared in two Super Bowl commercials. "The drivers are the stars," George Pyne, NASCAR's chief operating officer, told *USA Today*. "And Dale Jr. is the driver who transcends the sport."[3] The driver known as Junior is one of the new faces of NASCAR who appeal to a younger crowd. Among the other younger stars are Jimmie Johnson,

Ryan Newman, Kurt Busch, Kevin Harvick, Elliott Sadler, and Jamie McMurray.

Junior finished third in the 2003 NASCAR Cup series points standings. In 2004, he was in contention for the first Chase for the Championship before placing fifth. His career-high six victories in '04 were the second most in series, trailing only Jimmie Johnson's eight. In six full seasons racing in the Cup series, Earnhardt has collected an impressive 15 wins.

Following the terrorist attacks on New York City and Washington, D.C. on September 11, 2001, NASCAR's first Cup race was at Dover International Speedway in Delaware. A crowd of 140,000 was present on a bright sunny day. The track management gave everyone small American flags which they waved before the race with strong patriotic feelings. Dale Earnhardt Jr.'s victory in the race couldn't have been more popular with the fans. After circling the track in the reverse direction carrying a large American flag, Junior displayed his touch for saying the right thing. "I don't think it would have mattered who won this race," he said. "I'm just really fortunate to have been the guy. The fact that we're here, and we're racing and the fans can witness a good race is healing enough."[4]

Earnhardt's name gave him a start in NASCAR. His father was one of the sport's biggest stars. But, like other sons and younger brothers of famous drivers, he had to produce. Junior offered a strong hint about his racing skill when he won consecutive Busch Grand National series titles in 1998 and 1999. The Grand National series is one notch below the elite Nextel Cup series. The Busch series, as it is known in NASCAR, primarily is a developmental circuit. But at almost every race there are several Cup drivers on the track. Younger drivers like the presence of the Cup drivers because they can gauge their racing abilities against the best.

Fans express their patriotic feelings by waving American flags at the first NASCAR Cup race held after the terrorist attacks of September 11, 2001. Dale Earnhardt Jr. won this race, the Cal Ripken Jr. 400 at Dover International Speedway in Dover, Delaware.

Long before Dale Jr. and his father, Dale Sr., raced, NASCAR was a thriving sport. Led by Bill France Sr., NASCAR was founded in 1948. NASCAR's first race was in 1949 in Charlotte, North Carolina. NASCAR's first superspeedway race (more than one mile) was held in 1950 at Darlington Raceway in South Carolina. The racing pioneers in NASCAR included Lee Petty, Curtis Turner, Glenn "Fireball" Roberts, Buck Baker, and Tim and Fonty Flock. Races were held on the beach and roads in Daytona Beach, Florida until France built Daytona International Speedway. The new 2.5-mile Daytona track opened in 1959.

NASCAR's roots are in the southeastern United States. But by the late 1990s, NASCAR was racing all over the United States: in Texas, California, Chicago, and Kansas. NASCAR's television ratings are second only to the National Football League (NFL).

In 2000, Earnhardt's first full year in Cup, he didn't waste any time showing he was ready. At Texas Motor Speedway, north of Fort Worth, Texas, in just the season's seventh race, Earnhardt gained his first Cup victory. His father, a seven-time Cup champion, was there in victory lane to help Junior celebrate. Four races later, at Richmond, Virginia, Junior won again. NASCAR knew it had a new star in its racing stable. Junior didn't win again in 2000 and wound up 16th in the points standings. He was two places behind Matt Kenseth, the Cup Rookie of the Year. Junior admitted that, later in the year, his team couldn't maintain the lofty pace it set early in the season.

Junior chose the No. 8 for his bright red Budweiser Chevrolet because it's the number his father, Dale Sr., and grandfather, Ralph, carried on their short-track race cars. When NASCAR fans think of Dale Sr., they are more familiar with the black No. 3 Chevrolet that he drove in the 1980s until his death in a crash on the final lap of the 2001 Daytona 500. The black car fit Dale Sr.'s image as "The Intimidator," the driver whose aggressive style struck fear in the hearts of many racing rivals. Dale Sr.'s seven Cup titles are tied with Richard Petty for the most in NASCAR history. Earnhardt Sr.'s 76 race wins were the most among active drivers when he died. Overall, Earnhardt Sr. trailed only Petty (200), David Pearson (105), Bobby Allison and Darrell Waltrip (each 84) and Cale Yarborough (83).

Since his father's death, Junior has relied upon advice from several older NASCAR drivers. One of his mentors is Dale Jarrett. When Jarrett was starting in NASCAR in the mid-1980s, Dale Sr. was already established. Dale Sr.

Dale Earnhardt Sr., seven-time Cup winner, congratulates his son, Dale Earnhardt Jr., after "Junior" was presented with the Busch Series Championship trophy at Homestead-Miami Speedway on November 13, 1999.

provided racing and business tips for Jarrett. "His dad [Dale Sr.] was always there for me," Jarrett said. "He helped me in a lot of areas. I've just tried to do the same thing for Junior. I've known Junior since he was a kid. I've watched him come up . . . and make his mark in this sport, and then have to deal with something as tragic as losing his dad right when it seemed like things were going his way. I think Junior respects me. He can pick up the phone, come to my truck or my motor home and run something by me. He doesn't have to hold anything back. That's the kind of relationship I had with his dad."[5]

Dale Earnhardt Jr. talks to Dale Jarrett on pit road following a qualifying run at the Talladega Superspeedway. Jarrett has known Junior his whole life and has been a mentor to him since Dale Sr.'s death.

In July 2001 Junior won the first Cup race at Daytona following his father's death. It was an unbelievably emotional time for Junior and everyone connected with NASCAR. Hearts went out to Junior, imagining how he felt to win at the track where his father had died five months earlier. Junior was accustomed to having his father wrap an arm around his shoulder and hug him following race victories. Now, his father was only there in spirit. During the victory party, as Junior's thoughts drifted, he realized someone was standing near him. It was Dale Jarrett. The veteran driver stayed and talked until sunrise, making sure that the young race winner wasn't alone.

Talking about Jarrett and other experienced drivers, Junior said, "I can go to just about all the guys who raced with my daddy. I can go to Dale Jarrett and Bobby Labonte and even Rusty Wallace. If I've got a genuine question and they can see it in my eyes that I really care to know what they have to say, they're going to tell you. What it comes down to is respect. If you've got respect for those people and realize seniority and where you fit in on the ladder, people will treat you accordingly. I don't know that I've ever disrespected any of the veterans in the sport, so I can pretty much get a fair shake with just about all of them."[8]

The performances of Earnhardt and teammate Michael Waltrip at restrictor plate races at Daytona Beach, Florida, and Talladega, Alabama, are awesome. Between 2001 and '04 Dale Jr. and Waltrip won five of the eight races at Daytona. At Talladega in those years, they won six of eight, including four in a row by Dale Jr.

A restrictor plate is a thin, square piece of aluminum with four holes. The plates restrict airflow from the carburetor to the engine. The result is less horsepower and "slower" speeds. The intent is to make the races safer. Instead of racing at 200 miles per hour at the two superspeedways, car speeds run about 185 mph. However, many drivers dislike restrictor-plate races. When the field is close together at high speeds, restrictor plates often cause multi-car wrecks to occur.

DID YOU KNOW?

Dale Jr.'s favorite rock groups include 3 Doors Down, Korn, and the Matthew Good Band from Canada (since disbanded). Junior also is a big Elvis Presley fan.

Dale Jr.'s appeal to younger fans was evident during his several annual summer visits with the Urban Youth Racing School (UYRS) in Philadelphia, Pennsylvania. The UYRS encourages inner city young people to excel in school while also training them on weekends to polish their racing skills. Anthony Martin, the school's director, believes some of the school's students eventually will race in NASCAR. Several students have done internships with NASCAR teams, and some are in college, studying to be engineers. Through Anheuser-Busch, Martin arranged for Dale Jr. to stop in Philadelphia on his way to the second Cup race at Pocono Raceway. Surely it was impressive to the students when Junior arrived in a limousine. On one Philadelphia visit, Junior intended to race go kart-type cars on the wide roads in the city's historic Fairmount Park. Imagine one of NASCAR's star climbing into a small race car and dueling wheel to wheel with teenagers! The "race" didn't happen, however, because while warming up, one of the young drivers ran into a parked police car. Before he departed for the Pocono Mountains, Earnhardt was asked why he spent time with the city youths. Thinking for a moment or two, he replied, "I learn as much from them as they do from me."[7] That's typical of the thoughtful answers he usually provides.

Now that he is over 30, he thinks more about how his life is changing. At his Dale Earnhardt, Inc. headquarters in Mooresville, North Carolina, he said, "One day I'm going to walk in here and I won't be the 'party animal.' There will be a day when I want to get married and a day when I want to take some more time for myself. I will make some decisions that not everybody might like, but I think people will just have to understand. One thing I've learned is that you have to make yourself happy first."[8]

2

PAYING DUES IN THE EARLY YEARS

Dale Earnhardt Jr. was born October 10, 1974 in Concord, North Carolina. His mother, Brenda Gee Earnhardt, is Dale Earnhardt Sr.'s second wife. "Junior" has an older sister, Kelley, and an older brother, Kerry. Brenda's father, Robert, was involved in racing as a mechanic and fabricator.

After Dale Sr. and Brenda were divorced when Junior was three years old, he and his sister Kelley lived with their mother, now Brenda Jackson, in Virginia. When Dale Jr. was 10 and Kelley was 12 they moved back to Mooresville, North Carolina, to live with their father. Mooresville is 25 miles north of Charlotte. Junior describes Mooresville (population 20,000) as having a 1950s "Mayberry RFD" atmosphere. Junior likes Mooresville because it feels like home. If you want pizza in Mooresville, there's Pie-in-the-Sky. If you want a hamburger, there's What-A-Burger. Several NASCAR race teams, including Dale Earnhardt Inc. (DEI), are headquartered in Mooresville. Junior's father, the famed NASCAR driver, founded DEI. Other NASCAR Nextel Cup teams based in Mooresville include Penske South, Robert Yates Racing, and the Wood Brothers. The NASCAR Technical

Race car driving is in the Earnhardt blood. Aside from having a star driver as a father, Dale Earnhardt Jr.'s older half-brother, Kerry, pictured here, also drives in NASCAR.

Institute and the North Carolina Auto Racing Hall of Fame also are in Mooresville.

Dale Jr. attended Oak Ridge Military Academy in North Carolina for two years. As expected, he wasn't enthusiastic about the military routine, but he says it helped him mature.

Junior didn't meet his brother until he was in his mid-teens. Kerry's mother was Dale Sr.'s first wife. Kerry and Junior liked each other and eventually lived together in a double-wide trailer near their father's home. Of the three older Earnhardt children, Junior says that Kelley was the most promising racer among them. The three Earnhardt siblings competed in a late-model race in Nashville, Tennessee. On the first lap, all three were involved in a multi-car accident. Dale Jr. finished the race, but the cars that Kerry and Kelley were driving were too damaged to continue. Recalled Kerry, "It was a lot of fun racing with them. When you are racing with your brother and sister, you beat on them a little more and laugh when one of you passes the other. You enjoy it more than you would passing another driver on the track."[9]

Kelley is president of JR Motorsports, a company founded by Dale Jr. Her duties include handling his accounting, taxes, product endorsements, and payroll. She also takes care of fan requests and manages Junior's fan club and website. Following graduation from the University of North Carolina at Wilmington, Kelley received her business degree from the University of North Carolina-Charlotte.

After graduating from Mooresville Senior High School, Junior attended Mitchell Community College in Mooresville for two years. The school is known as "MIT": Mitchell, in

Junior's personal car collection includes two Corvettes (a 2001 and a 2005), a 2001 "Intimidator SS" Camaro, a 1996 Hummer, and a 2002 Mini Cooper. Junior's first race car was a 1978 Chevrolet Monte Carlo that he co-owned with his brother Kerry.

Dale Earnhardt Jr.'s older sister, Kelley, serves as the president of JR Motorsports, Junior's company.

Town. Later, he and Kerry worked at the Dale Earnhardt Chevrolet dealership in Newton, North Carolina. Junior's main job at the dealership was changing oil, while Kerry was a service writer. Earning $16,000 a year, Junior believes he did a good job. Eventually, however, he was fired when he asked if they would be paid overtime for attending a meeting after work.

In high school, Junior literally was the little brother. He was only 5-foot-4 inches. Kelley says she served as "mother hen" because he was picked on a lot in school. In his best-selling book, *Driver No. 8*, Junior said, "The Earnhardt name didn't carry any weight at school. Back then, nobody cared too much about who Dale Earnhardt was, although some-times I got teased on Monday if Dad did something like

Dale Earnhardt Jr., listens, as he often does, to "mother hen" and sister, Kelley at an event in Concord, North Carolina.

crash or run into another driver." Referring to their relationship, Kelley said, "He always had trust in me." Talking about her work, she said, "I love to be challenged, to be busy." She continued, "But working for Dale Jr. does present its challenges. As long as he isn't doing anything to hurt himself or illegal, I am very supportive of him. He knows he can talk to me [about personal issues]."[10]

Recalling his high school years, Junior told an interviewer that "it wasn't cool to be Dale Earnhardt's son."[11] He's not sure why—maybe the other students were jealous that he had a famous and wealthy father. Whatever the reason, Junior didn't feel accepted by the school athletes. After school, he cleaned out the stables on his father's farm. Junior thinks that the stable duties and working at his father's car dealership make him appreciate the enormous amounts of money and luxury he has now.

If he weren't Dale Earnhardt's son, he doesn't think he would be in racing. "I'd probably ended up working for the cotton mill or something," he said. Or else he thinks he'd be a mechanic in a car dealership. "When my mother turned custody of me and my sister over to my father in 1981, that's when my life changed," he recalled. "I didn't really know much about racing, nor was I even interested in it up to that point. That put me around my father and in the environment of NASCAR."[12]

Junior started racing go-karts when he was 12 years old. In *Driver No. 8* Junior said, "Dad thought racing a kart would be fun, so I got one and went out to set the world on fire. But karts don't have roll cages or seat belts, so most of the time I was being run over by or thrown off my own kart. After a few races, Dad decided that karts weren't safe enough and my karting career was over." Junior moved into racing late-model cars in the Charlotte area.

3

RISING IN RACING

After racing in NASCAR's late-model stock series from 1994 to 1996 and winning three feature races, Dale Jr. moved into the Busch Grand National series. His first race in the Busch series was in Myrtle Beach, South Carolina in 1996. He started seventh and finished 14th. During the 1997 season he made eight starts. His best finish was seventh at Michigan International Speedway. He was the second fastest qualifier in a Busch race at Bristol Motor Speedway in Tennessee. His first Busch victory was at Texas Motor Speedway in 1998 in just his 16th start in the series. The Texas track holds a fond place in Junior's heart because he also gained his first Cup series win on the 1.5-mile oval.

Junior settled into the Busch series, winning consecutive championships in 1998 and 1999. His overall Busch resume includes 18 victories and more than $3 million in earnings. In 1998, he won a series-leading seven races and had 16 top-five finishes. The next year he was just as strong, winning six races with 18 top-fives. By late in the '99 season, it was clear Junior was ready to try the Cup series. Understandably, he was nervous. Anheuser-Busch had signed him to a lucrative contract and promoted him as "The Rising Son." The multi-year deal was reportedly worth $10 million annually, an unheard-of

Anheuser-Busch sponsored Dale Earnhardt Jr. as a rookie for an estimated $10 million a year. Junior is pictured here awaiting the start of the 2001 Sharpie 500 at Bristol Motor Speedway.

amount for a rookie driver. When big money is involved, big things are expected. Sponsors generally aren't patient when they have invested big bucks in a driver and team.

"I know I have a lot of people watching me and wondering if I'm going to make it or flop," Junior said prior to the 2000 season. "Some people want me to be a big star because they pull for my dad and want me to be like him. Some people want me to fail because my dad's had so much success. But, I'm Dale Earnhardt Jr. I'm not my dad, and I have to be who I am."[13]

One person who originally opposed Junior's entry into the Busch series was his grandmother, Martha Earnhardt

(Dale Sr.'s mother). "I didn't think he was ready," she said. "I knew he had raced the smaller cars and all. But when they said they were going to put him in a Busch car, I said, 'This kid hasn't got enough experience.' Boy, he's proved me wrong. He's really something special."[14] Martha watched the Busch race that Junior won on television in her home in Kannapolis, North Carolina. "I was up in the middle of the floor, walking back and forth crying. I was a nervous wreck. I thought it was his father himself in that car driving. He's just amazing."[15]

Dale Sr. entrusted Tony Eury Sr. with guiding Junior on a daily basis as his crew chief in the Busch Grand National series, which is one level down from Nextel Cup. Tony Eury Jr. was Dale Jr.'s car chief. The relationship between the Earnhardts and Eurys began in the 1960s in Kannapolis. Ralph Earnhardt, Dale Jr.'s grandfather, and Ralph Eury were racers on the dirt tracks of North and South Carolina. Ralph Earnhardt won more than 250 races. He was good enough to make the list of NASCAR's top 50 drivers in the organization's first 50 years (1949–'99). Ralph Eury was a plumber. He did some work at Ralph Earnhardt's house and the two became friends. Earnhardt started building engines for Eury's race cars. Their children became friends.

The sometimes difficult relationship, especially between Dale Jr. and Tony Jr. in their Cup racing years reminded

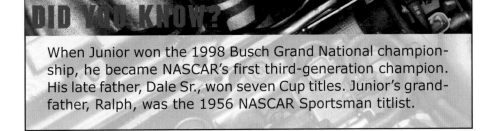

DID YOU KNOW?

When Junior won the 1998 Busch Grand National championship, he became NASCAR's first third-generation champion. His late father, Dale Sr., won seven Cup titles. Junior's grandfather, Ralph, was the 1956 NASCAR Sportsman titlist.

Fans and the media have cringed over the language Dale Earnhardt Jr. and Tony Eury Jr. use in their radio conversations, but the two men are like brothers. Earnhardt insists that each man respects the other a great deal.

people of a "family feud." Fans and media members who have listened in on their radio conversations during races have sometimes cringed over the language they heard. In 2003 Tony Jr. said:

> We have a relationship like two brothers. It's an "in the moment"-type deal. He's in a tense situation, and I'm in a tense situation, and everybody's got a lot of pressure to do well. We put pressure on each other to do well. One doesn't give up on the other. We respect each other a lot. Sometimes it comes across the wrong way, but it's nothing really serious. It's just like you'd do [with] your own brother.[16]

A year earlier, Dale Jr. said, "A lot of credit goes to Tony and Tony Jr. and the guys for keeping me well grounded. I get out of hand once in a while. They remind me that they're

Dale Earnhardt Jr. is a fan favorite. Junior is shown here signing autographs for fans after qualifying for the 2005 Aaron's 499 race at Talladega Superspeedway in Talladega, Alabama.

the ones working seven days a week and I'm the guy sitting at home on Mondays and Tuesdays. If I didn't act right, I don't know if Tony and the guys would have anything to do with me."[17]

Dale Sr. never rolled out the red carpet in racing for his younger son. Junior worked in the Chevrolet dealership that Dale Sr. owned, changing oil. After school, Junior cleaned out the stables on his father's farm. Dale Sr. wanted his son to understand that things shouldn't be handed to him just because his name was Earnhardt. But when Junior was ready to move into stock car racings big time, his father was impressed. "He's a young one," Dale Sr. said, "but he's handling it all pretty good. He's going wide open [on the track] with the guys and the team. I sit down and talk with him and see where his head is every once in a while. When I came into Cup, I had already beat up and down the road in the sportsman division. I spent my money until I was broke. I didn't have nothing. It's a little different [for Junior]. Things are there for him. His team, sponsors, things like that."[18]

Junior's fan appeal was immediately evident during his first full season in the Busch series in 1998. At Hickory Motor Speedway in North Carolina, fans lined up at his souvenir trailer three hours prior to the race. During what was intended to be a short stay, Junior posed for pictures and signed autographs. When grown women had difficulty speaking to him from shyness, he smiled and told them to enjoy the race. When white-haired men told him they cheered for his grandfather Ralph and his father and now were fans of his, Junior thanked them, saying, "That's real kind. I appreciate it."[19]

A grandmother with a glow, Martha Earnhardt said, "I've heard people say Dale Jr. is one of the nicest people they've ever met. And that makes me really proud when I hear those things, no matter what he does on the track."[20]

4

ROOKIE IN A RED CHEVROLET

After winning consecutive Busch Grand National series titles in 1998 and 1999, it was time for Junior, as he likes to be called, to make his full-time Winston Cup (now Nextel) debut. He would be driving the fire-engine red No. 8 Chevrolet, owned by Dale Earnhardt, Inc. (known in NASCAR as DEI). Crew chief Tony Eury moved with Junior from the Busch series to the Cup series. Tony's son, Tony Jr., also continued with the team. Tony Jr. is Dale Jr.'s cousin.

The first race of each Cup season is the Daytona 500. This race and the Indianapolis 500 are the two most famous races in the Unites States. Daytona will attract a crowd of about 150,000 in the grandstands and several thousand more in the infield. The Indy 500, in existence twice as long as Daytona, draws crowds of 350,000 to 400,000.

Dale Jr.'s first Daytona 500 as a Cup driver was the first he had seen in person. He had always been in school in February, so he had not been able to travel to Daytona Beach to see his famous father race. Since Junior was the focus of so much attention after winning two Busch series titles and carrying the Earnhardt name, he worried about even qualifying

Dale Earnhardt Jr. burns rubber on his famous red No. 8 Chevrolet after winning the 2004 NASCAR Nextel Cup series Golden Coral 500 at Atlanta Motor Speedway.

for the Daytona 500. Since he was a rookie, his team didn't have any owner's points from the previous season to fall back on. It was important to Junior to prove himself to the Cup veterans. Success in the Busch series doesn't guarantee success at the Cup level. Cup drivers are the best stock-car racers in the world. Several drivers who won races in the Busch series never made it big when they moved up to the Cup series. In the Daytona 500 Junior finished 13th after starting eighth. He beat his father, who finished 21st. Earnhardt's fans would have loved to eavesdrop on the family conversations after the race.

Perhaps the lowest point of Junior's rookie season occurred at Darlington Raceway in South Carolina. Darlington is one of the toughest tracks on the NASCAR circuit. NASCAR's original superspeedway, the 1.366-mile facility opened in 1950 and is known as "The Track Too Tough to Tame." Darlington's egg-shaped layout makes driving into and out of the corners difficult. Junior qualified 10th, but once the race started his car wouldn't handle the way it should. Near the end of the race, the car crashed into the wall. Junior's crew hurriedly repaired the damage, enabling him to return to the track. Finally, he drove into the garage area, parked the car and said he couldn't drive it. Tony Eury Sr., his crew chief, was not pleased and tried to find another driver who would finish the race in the car. Eury was unsuccessful, so Junior wound up a disappointing 40th. Returning to Mooresville, he was concerned that the team felt he had quit on them. The next day, however, the crew discovered that one of the rear axles on the car was broken. Junior felt better, because he was proven correct.

Two races later, Junior's mood brightened when he gained his first Cup victory in just his seventh start. He felt confident from the time he started practicing for the race at Texas Motor Speedway, north of Fort Worth. In some ways racers are like baseball or basketball players: sometimes they know warming up that they're going to have a good game. After qualifying fourth, Junior led four times in the race. He took the lead for the fifth and final time on lap 261 of the 334-lap race. Veterans Jeff Burton and Bobby Labonte were his biggest challengers in the homestretch of the race. Junior won by 5.9 seconds over runner-up Jeff Burton. As he drove through the final turn toward the start/finish line, he noticed the many flashbulbs popping in the grandstands. The cheering fans wanted to capture the special moment. Junior celebrated his breakthrough victory the way many racers do, creating a smokescreen with his tires. When he finally parked in victory lane, his father leaned into the car's cockpit and said, "I love you." Then Earnhardt Sr. added, "I want to make sure you take the time to enjoy this and enjoy what you accomplished today. You can get so swept up with what's going on around you that you really don't enjoy it yourself."[21]

Junior was very grateful that Gary Nelson, then the Cup series director, sat down with him before the Texas race. Nelson, a former Cup series crew chief, includes among his duties working with the rookie drivers. Nelson encouraged Junior, saying he thought he would be a good race car driver. That was the first time Junior received such positive feedback.

When Junior returned to DEI headquarters in Mooresville, a checkered flag was added to the American, North Carolina and DEI flags flying from flag poles. A checkered flag waves from the flagpole whenever a DEI team wins a race. The following Friday, when a smiling Junior arrived for the next race at Martinsville, Virginia, he was congratulated by many other drivers, crew members, and NASCAR officials. The kind thoughts made him feel very good. "It might be the best two hours of my life," he wrote in *Driver No. 8*, his best-selling book.

A few races later, at Richmond, Virginia, Junior became the first driver to win two races in 2000. Junior raced his father for the win late in the race, but Terry Labonte, another veteran, passed Earnhardt Sr. for second place. Junior held off Labonte for the victory. The only problem for Junior with winning was, he had to find his own way home. His father wouldn't hold his private jet until Junior finished his post-race interviews.

Another highlight of Junior's rookie season was winning The Winston, the all-star race held at Lowe's Motor

Speedway, near Charlotte, North Carolina. The Winston (now the NASCAR Nextel All-Star Challenge) does not count in the points standings. Only race winners are invited to The Winston, which is run in three segments. Junior has described the race as "an old-time Saturday night short-track shootout."[22] The prize money is substantial: $500,000 to the winner. The drivers also like the all-star race because most of them live in the Charlotte area, so they can commute to the track from their homes. After becoming the first rookie to win The Winston, Junior said he almost felt he was on the same level as his father as a racer. Junior dedicated the win to Adam Petty, a fourth generation Petty racer who was killed in May 2000 while practicing at New Hampshire International Speedway. After the race, Dale Earnhardt Sr. said, "I thought I could give [leader] Dale Jarrett some trouble, and then I saw this kid running in my rearview mirror and couldn't believe it. He just ran us down—he's something else."[23]

Junior was overwhelmed by the victory. "We had so many troubles that it is unbelievable to me that we're standing here in victory lane. We hit the wall . . . we had a left rear tire

Did you know? When Junior raced in the Pepsi 400 at Michigan International Speedway in 2000 with his father, Dale Sr., and brother, Kerry, it was just the second time that a father and two sons raced in the same Cup event. The Pettys were the first family to do so, when Lee Petty raced against his sons, Richard and Maurice.

Dale Earnhardt Jr. leads in his No. 8 car during the 2004 Nextel All-Star Challenge. Junior calls the race, "an old-time Saturday night short-track shootout."

come loose after the first segment. Despite all that we fought and fought and we ended up with such a great finish."[24]

Returning to The Winston a year later, Junior said, "I remember that at that time I could have quit driving race cars for the rest of my life and been happy. At that very moment, I felt like I would never enjoy another win as much." Referring to his father, who again celebrated with him in victory lane, Junior said, "He didn't have a plane he had to go jump on, so we threw beer on each other and jumped around and hollered and made fools of ourselves on national television. It was a lot of fun, a time I'll never forget."[25]

At the July race at Daytona, Junior met President George W. Bush. Junior joked that the president should feel comfortable, surrounded by the drivers who are predominantly Republicans.

A few weeks later, Junior was reminded how risky racing can be. While practicing for a 500-mile race at Pocono Raceway in Pennsylvania, he crashed. Traveling at about 170 miles per hour, his car rammed into the outer wall in Turn 2. Junior wasn't seriously injured, but because a track worker said he was temporarily unconscious (Junior denied this), he was transported to a hospital in nearby Allentown, Pennsylvania for tests. He was cleared and returned to the track. He finished 13th in the race.

Three races later, the Earnhardts—all three of them—made history by becoming the first father and two sons to start a Cup race since Lee Petty and sons Richard and Maurice did it in 1960. Kerry Earnhardt, Junior's half brother, qualified 27th, ahead of his father (37th). In the race though, Earnhardt Sr. finished sixth while Kerry was last. Junior, the fastest qualifier, finished a disappointing 31st.

Prior to the race at Talladega Superspeedway in Alabama, Junior received advice from veteran Dave Marcis on how to drive the longest track on the NASCAR schedule. Talladega is a high-banked 2.66-mile workout. Marcis reminded Junior that driving the car wide out of the corners, as drivers do on most oval tracks, is a mistake at Talladega. The track is so wide that if a driver does that, it adds extra distance to his runs and slows him down. After practicing taking the corners tighter, Junior qualified third. He led 24 laps late in the race, but the only lap that truly counts is the last lap. Junior finished 14th while his father won with a late charge.

In the season's final four races, Junior's highest finish was 13th, at Homestead, Florida. It was a disappointing conclusion for his rookie season. His racing pal, Matt Kenseth, finished 14th in the points standings to gain Rookie of the Year honors. Junior was 16th. While Junior wished he had

The three Earnhardt drivers Dale Jr. (left), Dale Sr. (center), and Kerry, are only the second father and two sons to start a Cup race. The first were Lee Petty and sons, Maurice and Richard, in 1960.

finished higher in the standings, knowing that he collected more than $2.6 million in prize money soothed his feelings a little. At least Dale Earnhardt Sr. had a season to smile about. A seven-time Cup champion, he was runner-up to champion Bobby Labonte in points.

As the 2000 season ended, Junior felt more professional. "I discovered that communication is a two-way street," he wrote in his book *Driver No. 8.* "I didn't always talk things out when I should, and sometimes I got [mad] and sulked when I should have worked to find a solution. In truth, I'm happy Tony Sr. had enough confidence in me and didn't slug me in the face when I wasn't acting my age."

5

MATURING THROUGH TRAGEDY

In 2001, the elation of Michael Waltrip's first Cup victory in 463 starts abruptly vanished minutes after Waltrip pulled into victory lane at Daytona International Speedway. Waltrip was driving his first race for Dale Earnhardt Inc., known in NASCAR as DEI. Despite Waltrip's winless record for 16 years, Dale Earnhardt Sr. had hired him in the off season. Finally driving for a top NASCAR team, Waltrip was elated over the opportunity. That joy quickly vanished, however, when Earnhardt crashed on the final lap of the Daytona 500. Nine out of 10 times after such an accident, a driver climbs out of his car, waves to the crowd and walks away, ready to race again. Sadly, this was the rare time when the driver didn't survive. Those at the race will forever remember Earnhardt's younger son, Dale Jr., running toward Turn 4 where his father's car had stopped. Dale Jr. had finished second in the race to Waltrip, his DEI teammate. Many observers believe that Earnhardt was helping Waltrip by blocking other cars when the crash occurred.

At the time of the accident, Junior was still a "kid." He was 26, fresh from a successful Cup rookie season. He was

Dale Earnhardt Sr.'s car is shown breaking apart after being hit by Ken Schrader's No. 36 car during the final lap of the Daytona 500 on February 18, 2001. Sadly, Earnhardt Sr. did not survive the crash.

enjoying racing with his father. They were looking forward to several more years of competing against each other and spending time together at the racetracks. Racing with Junior rejuvenated his father's career. Dale Sr. was a seven-time Cup champion, but he hadn't won a championship since 1994. Between 1986 and 1994 Dale Sr. won six of his seven titles (the other was in 1980). During this time, Dale Sr. built his reputation as "The Intimidator." When his black No. 3 Chevrolet appeared in a competitor's rear view mirror, many other drivers suddenly grew very nervous. Earnhardt was a master at weaving past rivals, either with no contact or by bumping them out of the way.

From 1995 through 1999, Dale Sr. was still a major factor in the Cup series. He won 11 races and finished from second ('95) to eighth ('98) in the points standings. That's a record that many drivers would trade in their private jets to have. But when you are used to winning championships, it's not enough.

Speaking with former Cup champion Darrell Waltrip, an analyst for Fox Sports, shortly after Dale Sr.'s death, Junior said, "I do a lot of things that I never did before, and I only do them because I know he wanted me to do them." The nationwide reaction to his father's death surprised Junior. "[People] must have said to themselves, 'Man, this guy meant a lot to a lot of people; tell me a little bit about this guy,'" Junior said. "It makes me feel good to see what he meant to so many people."

Before the 2001 race at Texas Motor Speedway, then teammate Steve Park said: "I've seen incredible changes in Dale." The race in Texas was just the sixth after Dale Sr. died. "He went from being a young man to being a grown man in one weekend. He's just done a tremendous job in going from wanting to sit home and listen to CDs to helping run a multimillion-dollar company," Park said.[26]

Some of the sadness enveloping Junior since his father's death was lifted when he returned to Daytona in July 2001 and won the 400-mile race. The victory brought smiles to the faces of everyone at Dale Earnhardt Inc. (DEI) and those involved with NASCAR. By now, Junior was a very popular driver, perhaps the most popular in NASCAR. Even those who weren't his fans were happy for him. In the fall of 2001, he said, "I surprised myself to come back and win at

Dale Earnhardt Jr. celebrates his Pepsi 400 victory in Victory Lane on July 7, 2001.

Daytona." Referring to the first race after the terrorist attacks of September 2001, Junior said, "And then for us to be able to [win] at Dover after everything that happened: We won two races in strange circumstances and I was really proud of that. It appears to me that I've proved I can handle those situations and then go perform."[27]

Looking back at his rookie year in the Cup series, Junior said, "Last year seems like five years ago almost. It was a really hard year. It was a lot tougher transition coming from the Busch to the Cup series than I anticipated. This year, it seems like it's easier to take things in stride and to be able to concentrate on the next day or the next project."[28] As all drivers are, Junior is aware of the cheers he hears when he is introduced before races. "It's an overwhelming experience. That's probably 50 percent of my motivation to get into the car right before a race. When I hear that, I am ready to go."[29]

An example of how he thinks about other things than racing is this comment he made in July 2001. Then 26 years old, he said, "I don't really take things that seriously. I don't know why. But it seems it's a lot easier to deal with it that way because things change, and it's easier to let go of the stuff if you don't get too attached to it."[30] He is considered colorful by many. There's no doubt there is a sizzle about him. He's into rock music big time, but he also has his quiet moments. While Junior has grown into acknowledging the passionate support of fans, there are still times he prefers staying out of the limelight. Hanging out with friends he has known since high school is one of his joys in life. The day after Christmas 2001, Junior and three friends headed to Buffalo, New York, to help a friend move to the Carolinas. The friend wanted to get into racing. The trip took 22 hours. On the way back, they stopped in Gettysburg, Pennsylvania, and scouted the Civil War battlefield. "It was about 2 [o'clock] in the morning, so it was kind of hard to see what was going on," Junior said.[31] The return trip detoured to Ohio, where they spent a night. While eating dinner at a restaurant/bar, some people recognized Junior and a crowd gathered. Junior didn't mind. "We just had a good time," he said. "It was kind of cool to get away and be normal for a little while."[32]

Dale Earnhardt Jr. accepts the Winston Cup Series award for 8th place at the season-ending awards banquet in New York City.

Junior's 2001 season was an improvement over his rookie year, indicating that he had the potential to be a contender every year in the Cup series. He won three races—at Daytona in July, at Dover in September, and at Talladega, Alabama in October. He finished eighth in the points standings, earning a place on the stage at the Waldorf-Astoria Hotel in New York City for NASCAR's season-ending awards banquet. A sign of the prosperous times in NASCAR was Junior's earnings for the year: $5.8 million, more than his late father ever earned in a season. Junior's prize money included a $1 million bonus at Talladega as part of Winston's No Bull program.

In 2002, Junior slipped a little, winning only two races and finishing 11th in the points standings. His two victories were at Talladega, where DEI cars reigned supreme. Junior's father is the all-time winner at Talladega with 10 wins. DEI personnel have figured out how to win at the Talladega and Daytona superspeedways (2.5-mile and longer tracks). These are the only two tracks where restrictor plates are used in the engines to slow down the cars. Although Junior didn't win as many races as he would have liked in 2002, he led the most laps (1,068) and posted a career-high top-5 finishes (11). When drivers regularly run up front, they figure they'll eventually win races.

Junior proved again during the 2003 season that he had established himself as one of the Cup series premier drivers. His third-place finish in the points chase was his career-best. He was 207 points off the pace of champion Matt Kenseth. Junior extended his winning streak at Talladega to four in a

DID YOU KNOW?

Kelley Earnhardt, Dale Jr.'s sister and the president of his JR Motorsports company, is married to Jimmy Elledge. He is the crew chief for Casey Mears, driver of the No. 41 Dodge. Elledge previously worked for drivers Dale Jarrett, Bobby Hamilton, and Kenny Wallace.

row. He also won at Phoenix, Arizona. During the 36-race schedule, Junior was second in the points standings for more than half the year: 19 weeks. Among his other career bests were 13 top-5 finishes and 21 top-10s.

By 2003, with more than 100 Cup races behind him, Junior was feeling more comfortable with his celebrity status. "I'm trying to be more understanding of my responsibilities," he said. "You get a year older, more experienced, that always makes you better. I guess I appreciate people noticing, although I don't know any other drivers whose maturity level is being documented at this point like mine is." He said he keeps his father in his thoughts and still tries to please him. He often thinks: what would Dad do? "Sometimes I do feel that way," he said. "It's like he would be disappointed in me if I didn't buckle down."[33]

Jeff Gordon, a four-time Cup champion who also achieved racing success at a young age, admires the way Junior has handled his fame. "He was whisked into this sport awful fast and it's going to take some time [to settle in], especially when your last name is Earnhardt," Gordon said. "He's getting his priorities straight and things are falling into place for him. I think Dale should be proud of that."[34]

6

CHANGES FOR
THE TEAM

Under the new Chase format, after the first 26 races of the 2004 season, the top 10 drivers were separated by increments of five points. Only the top 10 drivers were eligible for the championship. Earnhardt won two of the 10 Chase races, at Talladega, Alabama, and Phoenix, Arizona. After his Talladega victory, Earnhardt temporarily led the Chase by 13 points over Kurt Busch. However, NASCAR penalized Earnhardt 25 points for saying a swearword in a post-race television interview. The penalty dropped Earnhardt 12 points behind Busch, the eventual champion. Earnhardt remained in second place through the next two races. But consecutive 33rd-place finishes pushed Earnhardt to fifth in the standings. Winning at Phoenix elevated him to third, 47 points behind the leader, close enough to still have a chance at his first title. However, two disappointing finishes in the last two races—11th at Darlington and 23rd at Homestead, Florida—spoiled his championship hopes.

Looking ahead to the 2005 season, Junior offered these thoughts about what he and his team learned during the first Chase for the Championship. "You don't have to take the first

26 races so seriously," he said. "You can really enjoy the season [and] enjoy yourself. You can go out there and have fun racing. If you're a good enough team, you'll make the top 10. I think where my team is now, we can make it with no problem."[35]

The 2004 racing season was eventful for Junior in several ways. He began the year by winning the Daytona 500, traditionally the most important race on the NASCAR schedule. It was just Junior's fifth start in the Daytona 500. His late father raced in 19 Daytona 500s before winning in 1998. The Daytona 500 is regarded as the "Super Bowl" of stock car racing. Most sports conclude their seasons with their most important events. NASCAR is different. The Daytona 500, first run in 1959, is held in February because the weather in Florida is reasonably warm. Race fans from colder parts of the country are lured to Daytona to watch the race. The Daytona 500 also generates the top television ratings of the year for a NASCAR race. The event sets the tone for the rest of the year. After winning the 500, Junior said:

> I'm just real excited to have won this race. It's really hard to win it. Some of our greatest competitors come in and out of this sport without taking this trophy home. Things that have happened here affected so many people who are real close to me. Every time we come to Daytona, we just feel real strong about being here.[36]

Junior went on to win five more races in 2004. His total of six victories was second only to Jimmie Johnson's eight. Three races after Daytona, Junior won at Atlanta. He followed with victories at Richmond, Virginia; Bristol, Tennessee; Talladega, Alabama; and Phoenix, Arizona. After the eighth race of the season, Junior led the points race. He maintained his lead through the next six races. Junior finished fifth in the points standings, 138 points behind winner Kurt Busch.

Dale Earnhardt Jr. holds his trophy high after his 2004 Daytona 500 victory.

Junior's triumph at Talladega Superspeedway on October 3 should have given him a 13-point lead over Kurt Busch in the Chase for the Championship. However, NASCAR deducted 25 points from his collection and fined him $10,000 for cursing during a post-race television interview. What he said was relatively tame by today's standards, but NASCAR officials strongly believed that his choice of words was not appropriate for a live television interview. After winning his

Dale Earnhardt Jr. leads during the final lap of the EA Sports 500 at Talladega Superspeedway. Junior was penalized for inappropriate language during a live television post-race interview.

fifth race in 10 career starts at Talladega, Junior was asked what it meant to win that often at the 2.66-mile high-banked speedway. "Well, it don't mean *bleep* right now," he replied. "Daddy's won here 10 times, so I've got to do more winning."[37]

While many observers agreed that Junior's remark out of line, they questioned NASCAR's decision to influence the points race. Cup racing rival Tony Stewart stood up for Junior, saying, "I think we're starting to nitpick and scrutinize way too much in this series. Since when does something that somebody says have an effect on winning the championship? What he said didn't cheat anybody on the race track. It didn't have any effect on how the race was run. That [penalty] can have an effect on millions of dollars and how their sponsors have to handle this now. It's been totally unfair to him and his race team."[38] Another reason that NASCAR penalized Junior with a points deduction was to avoid criticism that NASCAR favors Junior. Some critics believe that Junior is treated with kid gloves because he is Dale Earnhardt Sr.'s son and a fan favorite. This is a charge that Junior strongly disputes. Appearing on the Speed Channel show "Wind Tunnel," Junior said, "NASCAR couldn't run a legitimate business if there was a teacher's pet. I think it's fair to say that I'm watched pretty closely by NASCAR. There is a bunch of us in the series that maybe needs a little extra attention. I think NASCAR has been fair in all of their judgments."

Junior had a scary and painful experience during July. With no Cup race on a weekend, Junior decided to race a Corvette in an American LeMans series race in California. While practicing for the race at Infineon Raceway (formerly Sears Point Raceway) in Sonoma, his car spun in Turn 8 of the 1.99-mile road course and struck a barrier. When the car caught on fire, Junior managed to climb out. But he sustained second-degree burns on his chin and legs. Later, in an interview with the CBS show "60 Minutes" he said he thought his father's spirit helped him escape from the burning car. Said Junior: "I think he had a lot to do with me getting out of the car. I don't want to put some weird psycho twist on it, like he was pulling me out, but he had a lot to do with me getting out of that car." The feeling of receiving assistance was so clear to Junior that when he was in the raceway's infield care center, he asked Steve Crisp, the public relations person with him for the weekend, if the person who helped rescue him was ever found. According to Junior, Crisp insisted that no one helped get him out of the car. "That's strange," Junior said, "because I swear somebody had me underneath my arms and was carrying me out of the car. It was as real as [it could be]."

Dale Earnhardt Jr. climbs out of his flaming Corvette CS-P after an accident on July 18, 2004, in Sonoma, California.

The pain and discomfort caused by the burns forced Junior to climb out of his race car after starting the next two races, at New Hampshire International Speedway and Pocono Raceway. At New Hampshire, he was replaced by Martin Truex Jr., who won the 2004 Busch Grand National Series driving for Dale Earnhardt, Inc. Truex finished 31st. At Pocono, veteran driver John Andretti finished the race, in 25th place. Junior was credited with the finishes in both races because NASCAR rules say that drivers who start races receive the points.

Following the 2004 season, Dale Earnhardt, Inc. shuffled personnel. Tony Eury Sr. is now director of competition, overseeing DEI's three Nextel Cup and two Busch Grand National Series teams. Tony Jr. is Michael Waltrip's crew chief. Peter Rondeau, who had served as Waltrip's crew chief for the final few races of the 2004 season, took over as Dale Jr.'s crew chief.

Tony Eury Sr., Dale Earnhardt Jr.'s director of competition, listens to Junior following a practice session at Daytona International Speedway.

To make the changes, Richie Gilmore, DEI's vice president of motorsports, had to get Dale Jr.'s approval. Junior had often said that he and the Eurys would race together "forever." Junior knew that Tony Jr. was ready to be a Cup crew chief. "This will allow him to mature a lot," Dale Jr. said. "I've always worked with family and answered to family. Working with different people will allow me to learn the respect side. I was a good race car driver, but I wasn't necessarily a professional about how I was on the radio."[39]

As he has grown older, Junior believes he has gotten better at handling fame and his role with DEI. In 2003 he said,

"I'm trying to be more understanding of my responsibilities. You get a year older, more experienced, that always makes you better."[40]

By the start of the 2005 season, Junior was feeling even more comfortable with his role in racing and as a celebrity. "I've already done more than I thought I would," he said. "I've already got more money and more victories than I ever thought I would. To me, it's amusing sometimes to hear what people think you can do or should do, because I'm way past what I thought I could do. There's a sense of satisfaction that comes with everybody having all the expectations on you and you meeting at least a large percentage of it." Junior still maintains that he is basically a shy person. "I feel I miss out on a lot of stuff because I'm kind of a shy guy." Referring to Jeff Gordon's appearances on such television shows as "Regis and Kelly" and "Saturday Night Live," Junior said, "To do something like 'Saturday Night Live' and stuff like that, [it's] amazing that Jeff had the guts to do that. I'd never be able to do that. I turn down a lot of things. I've been on 'Leno' and I still turn it down sometimes, because I'm just too nervous to go on there."[41]

Junior is co-owner of Chance 2 Motorsports, a successful Busch Grand National team. Driving for Chance 2, Martin Truex Jr. won the 2004 Busch series championship as a rookie. Teresa Earnhardt, Junior's stepmother, is the other owner of Chance 2.

Richard Childress owned the cars driven by Dale Earnhardt Sr. Childress now owns the Cup cars driven by Kevin Harvick, Jeff Burton and Dave Blaney. Beyond their business relationship, Childress and Dale Sr. were good friends. Childress has enjoyed watching Dale Jr. mature. "I've seen him get a lot more comfortable with his role," Childress said prior to the 2005 Daytona 500. "I think the thing he's come to realize is that not only do you love what you do, driving the race cars and all, but along with that comes some commitment. You've got to be committed to the fans and the sport, and he's really turned the corner. Seeing him mature has been great. Seeing the success he's had really brings pleasure."[42]

Halfway through the 26-race regular season of 2005, however, it became clear that the preseason shake-up had not produced the desired results. Pete Rondeau was fired after only 11 races as crew chief. Some saw this as a panic move. For the first time since 1999, Dale Jr. was winless. He failed to earn a pole. He had two flat tires in the Pocono 500 and finished 33rd. "It's hard to find anything positive about a day like today," Junior commented after the race. "You have to be careful not to make things worse than they are. There's a big difference between understanding what you need to improve and beating yourself up about it … I see it as a very steep mountain, but I'm in it to win it."[43]

Given Dale Jr.'s experience and commitment to the sport, no one doubts that he will get through this rough patch and be back in victory lane before long.

NOTES

Chapter 1

1. Joe Macenka, "'Little E' signs long-term deal with Budweiser." *Associated Press*, 1998.

2. Ibid.

3. Bruce Horovitz, "Dale Jr. zooms to front of pack in endorsements." *USA Today*, February 12, 2004. *www. usatoday.com/money/advertising/2004-02-12-dalejr_ x.htm.*

4. Dale Earnhardt Jr., post-race press conference (Dover, DE), September 24, 2001.

5. Dave Kallmann, "Jarrett still standing alongside Junior." *Milwaukee Journal Sentinel*, February 24, 2004. *www. jsonline.com/sports/race/feb04/208852.asp.*

6. Conference call with Dale Earnhardt Jr., May 25, 2004.

7. Dale Earnhardt Jr., press conference, Philadelphia, PA, July 2001.

8. David Poole, "Earnhardt Jr. maturing, gaining confidence." *Charlotte Observer*, October 2001.

Chapter 2

9. Meghan Frazier, "The History of . . . Kerry Earnhardt: 'My Confidence Level Is Building And Getting Better Every Week.'" *Stock Car Racing. www.stockcarracing.com/thehistoryof/78519/index.html.*

10.   Jim Utter, "Kelley Earnhardt still plays the role of big sister well." ThatsRacin.com, January 31, 2003. *www.thatsracin.com/mld/thatsracin/5075198.htm?template =contentModules/printstory.jsp.*

11.   "The Playboy Interview: Dale Earnhardt Jr." *Playboy,* September 2001.

12.   Conference call with Dale Earnhardt Jr., October 1, 2002.

Chapter 3

13.   Mike Harris, "Earnhardt Jr. nervous about Winston Cup debut." *Associated Press,* May 13, 1999. *http:// augustasports.com/stories/051399/oth_ 251-5091.000.shtml.*

14.   Joe Macenka, "Another Earnhardt making a name for himself." *Associated Press,* April 16, 1998. *http: // archives.pottsville.com/archives/1998/Apr/17/ D125979.htm.*

15.   Ibid.

16.   Marty Smith, "Conversation: Tony Eury Jr." *Turner Sports Interactive,* March 26, 2003. *www.nascar. com/2003/news/features/conversation/03/26/teuryjr_ convo/.*

17.   Dale Earnhardt Jr., post-race press conference (Talladega, AL), April 21, 2002.

18.   Jim Utter, "Son's rise surprises Earnhardt." *Charlotte Observer,* May 25, 1999.

19.   Joe Macenka, "Another Earnhardt making a name for himself."

20. Ibid.

Chapter 4

21. Dale Earnhardt Jr. and Jade Gurss. *Driver No. 8*. New York, NY: Warner Books, 2002.

22. Ibid.

23. Jenna Fryer, "Junior returns to sit of greatest thrill." *Associated Press*, May 2000.

24. Ibid.

25. "Earnhardt Jr. says he'll never forget Winston victory." *Associated Press*, May 18, 2001. *http://sports illustrated.cnn.com/motorsports/2001/cocacola600/ news/2001/05/16/littlee_winston_ap/*.

Chapter 5

26. Conference call with Dale Earnhardt Jr., April 2001.

27. Conference call with Dale Earnhardt Jr., October 2001.

28. Conference call with Dale Earnhardt Jr., July 2001.

29. David Poole, "Earnhardt Jr. maturing, gaining confidence."

30. Conference call with Dale Earnhardt Jr., July 2001.

31. David Poole, "Earnhardt Jr. enjoyed time off." *Charlotte Observer*, January 15, 2002.

32. Ibid.

33. Steve Ballard, "Earnhardt Jr. grows into a name." *Indianapolis Star*, August 3, 2003. *www.suntimes. com/output/racing/cst-spt-brick03.html.*

34. Ibid.

Chapter 6

35. Conference call with Dale Earnhardt Jr., Fall 2004.

36. Dale Earnhardt Jr., post-race press conference, February 15, 2004, Daytona 500.

37. Dale Earnhardt Jr., post-race television interview (Talladega, AL), NBC Sports, October 3, 2004.

38. Mike Harris, "Stewart backs Earnhardt on NASCAR penalty (phillyburbs.com)." *Associated Press*, October 9, 2004. *www.phillyburbs.com/pb-dyn/news/ 49-10102004-380319.html.*

39. Dale Earnhardt Jr., press conference prior to Daytona 500, February 2005.

40. Steve Ballard, "Earnhardt Jr. grows into a name."

41. Mike Harris, "Earnhardt Jr. grows into his starring role." *Associated Press*, February 17, 2005. *www.sacbee.com/24hour/sports/racing/stock/story/ 2161756p-10235733c.html.*

42. Ibid.

43. Gary Graves, "Earnhardt's season spinning out of control." *USA Today*, June 13, 2005.

CHRONOLOGY

1974 Dale Jr. is born October 10, 1974 in Concord, North Carolina.

1975 Dale Jr.'s father, Dale Earnhardt Sr., makes his NASCAR Winston Cup debut in the World 600 at Charlotte Motor Speedway.

1979 Dale Sr. is named Winston Cup Rookie of the Year.

1980 Dale Sr. wins his first of a record-tying seven Cup driving championships.

1986 Dale Jr. races in a go-kart for the first time.

1991 Dale Jr. starts racing in the street-stock division at Concord Motorsport Park near Charlotte.

1994 Dale Jr. begins racing in late model stock cars in Charlotte area tracks.

1996 Dale Jr. makes his NASCAR Busch Grand National debut at Myrtle Beach, South Carolina.

1997 Dale Jr. signs a $10 million per year deal with Anheuser-Busch. "Junior" gains the Busch Series points championship (seven wins).

1998 Dale Jr. repeats as the Busch champion (six wins). Also makes his Winston Cup debut in the Coca-Cola 600 at Charlotte Motor Speedway.

1999 In his first full season in the Cup series Junior wins two races and finishes 16th in points.

2000 Dale Jr. finishes eighth in the points standings (three wins).

2001 Dale Jr. finishes 11th in the points standings (two wins). One of his victories was in the July race at Daytona, the first race at the track after his father died in a last-lap crash in the Daytona 500 in February.

2002 Posts career-best third-place finish in the points chase (two wins).

2003 His six victories are second only to Jimmie Johnson's eight. Junior is fifth in points.

2004 Junior won six Cup races, second only to Jimmie Johnson's series-leading eight victories. One of Junior's victories was the Daytona 500. He finished fifth in the points standings and was voted NASCAR's Most Popular Driver for the second consecutive year.

2005 The season began on a positive note with a third-place finish in the Daytona 500. However, a series of disappointing finishes dropped Junior out of the top 10 in points prior to the halfway mark of the season.

STATISTICS

Dale Earnhardt Jr.

Year	Races	Wins	Top 5	Top 10	Poles	Rank	Money Won
1999	5	0	0	1	0	48	$162,095
2000	34	2	3	5	2	16	$2,801,881
2001	36	3	9	15	2	8	$5,827,542
2002	36	2	11	16	2	11	$4,970,034
2003	36	2	13	21	0	3	$6,980,807
2004	36	6	16	21	0	5	$8,906,860
Total	183	15	52	79	6		$29,549,219

FURTHER READING

Edelstein, Robert. *NASCAR Generations: The Legacy of Family in NASCAR Racing*. New York, NY: Harper Entertainment, 2000.

Fleischman, Bill, and al Pearce. *The Unauthorized NASCAR Fan Guide 2004*. Detroit, MI: Visible Ink Press, 2004.

Gillespie, Tom. *I Remember Dale Earnhardt: Personal Memories of and Testimonials to Stock Car Racing's Most Beloved Driver (as told by the people who knew him best)*. Nashville, TN: Cumberland House, 2001.

Mayne, Kevin. *The Dale Earnhardt Story*. New York, NY: ESPN Books, 2004.

Montville, Leigh. *At the Altar of Speed: The Fast Life and Tragic Death of Dale Earnhardt*. New York, NY: Doubleday, 2001.

BIBLIOGRAPHY

Ballard, Steve. "Earnhardt Jr. grows into a name." *Indianapolis Star*, August 3, 2003. *www.suntimes.com/ output/racing/cst-spt-brick03.html.*

Earnhardt Jr., Dale. Conference call, April 2001.

———. Conference call, July 2001.

———. Conference call, October 2001.

———. Conference call, October 1, 2002.

———. Conference call, May 25, 2004.

———. Conference call, Fall 2004.

———. Post-race press conference (Dover, DE), September 24, 2001.

———. Post-race press conference (Talladega, AL), April 21, 2002.

———. Post-race press conference (Daytona Beach, FL), February 15, 2004.

———. Post-race television interview (Talladega, AL). NBC Sports, October 3, 2004.

———. Press conference, (Concord, NC), May 2000.

———. Press conference (Philadelphia, PA) July 2001.

———. Press conference (Daytona Beach, FL), February 2005.

Earnhardt Jr., Dale, and Jade Gurss. *Driver No. 8*. New York, NY: Warner Books, 2002.

"Earnhardt Jr. says he'll never forget Winston victory." *Associated Press*, May 18, 2001. *http://sportsillustrated.cnn.com/motorsports/2001/cocacola600/news/2001/05/16/littlee_winston_ap/*.

Frazier, Meghan. "The History of . . . Kerry Earnhardt: 'My Confidence Level Is Building And Getting Better Every Week." *Stock Car Racing. www.stockcarracing.com/thehistoryof/78519/index.html.*

Harris, Mike, "Earnhardt Jr. grows into his starring role." *Associated Press*, February 17, 2005. *www.sacbee.com/24hour/sports/racing/stock/story/2161756p-10235733c.html.*

———. "Earnhardt Jr. nervous about Winston Cup debut." *Associated Press*, May 13, 1999. *http://augustasports.com/stories/051399/oth_251-5091.000.shtml.*

———. "Stewart backs Earnhardt on NASCAR penalty (phillyburbs.com)." *Associated Press*, October 9, 2004. *www.phillyburbs.com/pb-dyn/news/49-10102004-380319.html.*

Horovitz, Bruce. "Dale Jr. zooms to front of pack in endorsements." *USA Today*, February 12, 2004. *www.usatoday.com/money/advertising/2004-02-12-dalejr_x.htm.*

Kallmann, Dave. "Jarrett still standing alongside Junior." *Milwaukee Journal Sentinel*. February 24, 2004. *www.jsonline.com/sports/race/feb04/208852.asp.*

Macenka, Joe. "Another Earnhardt making a name for himself." *Associated Press*, April 16, 1998. *http://archives. pottsville.com/archives/1998/Apr/17/D125979.htm.*

———. "'Little E' signs long-term deal with Budweiser." *Associated Press*, 1998.

"The Playboy Interview: Dale Earnhardt Jr." *Playboy.* September 2001.

Poole, David. "Earnhardt Jr. enjoyed time off", *Charlotte Observer*, January 15, 2002.

———. "Earnhardt Jr. maturing, gaining confidence." *Charlotte Observer*, October 2001.

Smith, Marty. "Conversation: Tony Eury Jr." *Turner Sports Interactive*, March 26, 2003. *www.nascar.com/2003/ news/features/conversation/03/26/teuryjr_convo/.*

Utter, Jim. "Kelley Earnhardt still plays the role of big sister well." ThatsRacin.com, January 31, 2003. *www. thatsracin.com/mld/thatsracin/5075198.htm?template= contentModules/printstory.jsp.*

———. "Son's rise surprises Earnhardt." *Charlotte Observer*, May 25, 1999.

ADDRESSES

NASCAR
P.O. Box 2875
Daytona Beach, FL 32120
(386) 253-0611

Dale Earnhardt, Inc.
1675 Dale Earnhardt Highway 3
Mooresville, NC 28115
(704) 662-8000

INTERNET SITES

www.dalejr.net

This site contains information about Dale Earnhardt Jr. and his racing team, including a fan center and message board.

www.daleearnhardtinc.com

This site provides information about Dale Earnhardt Inc. (DEI), including the Michael Waltrip No. 15 team.

www.nascar.com

This site offers information on the top three NASCAR racing series: Nextel Cup, Busch Grand National, and Craftsman Truck Series.

Photo Credits:

INDEX

ABOUT THE AUTHOR

Bill Fleischman is a veteran *Philadelphia Daily News* sports writer. He has covered auto racing, college basketball, the National Hockey League and tennis. He is co-author of *The Unauthorized NASCAR Fan Guide 2004*. He is former president of the Philadelphia Sports Writers Association and the Professional Hockey Writers Association. He is an adjunct professor in the University of Delaware journalism program. A graduate of Gettysburg College, Fleischman and his wife, Barbara, live in Wilmington, Delaware.